Gigi's Starting School

Author Yvonne V. Cabrera-Perez

Illustrations By Monique Turchan

Copyright © 2018 Yvonne V. Cabrera-Perez
Illustrated by Monique Turchan
All rights reserved.

Psalm 55:22

No part of this book may be reproduced in any manner without the written consent of the publisher except for brief excerpts in critical reviews or articles.

ISBN: 978-1-61244-638-7
Library of Congress Control Number: 2018905446

Printed in the United States of America

Halo Publishing International
1100 NW Loop 410
Suite 700 - 176
San Antonio, Texas 78213
1-877-705-9647
www.halopublishing.com
contact@halopublishing.com

To my husband, Danny, and my children Daniel, Michael, and Gianna: Thank you for supporting, encouraging, and inspiring me to live my dreams. This is for you!

To my mom and dad: Thank you for the sacrifices you've made.

To the students I've had the pleasure of experiencing the first day of school with: Thank you for the memories!

Gigi gives a great, big yawn, rubs her eyes, and stretches out her little arms. Gigi's feelings aren't glad. The day has come, and she feels sad!

Gigi tells her mommy, "I don't want to go to school. I'm gonna miss you!"

"Yes, it's true," says Gigi's mommy. "School is starting for little big girls just like you. I will miss you, too!"

Gigi dresses in a colorful shirt, matching her new, flowered skirt. She puts on her brand new shoes. Gigi's feeling very blue!

Gigi tells her mommy, "I don't want to go to school. I'm gonna miss you!"

"Yes, it's true," says Gigi's mommy. "School is starting for little big girls just like you. I will miss you, too!"

Gigi brushes her teeth and washes her face. Gigi's feeling in a daze! Mommy combs her hair and makes a braid. Gigi's feeling very afraid!

Gigi tells her mommy, "I don't want to go to school. I'm gonna miss you!"

"Yes, it's true," says Gigi's mommy. "School is starting for little big girls just like you. I will miss you, too!"

Gigi's breakfast is ready. It's time to eat. She pulls up her little seat. Gigi's food doesn't look too yummy! Gigi's tummy feels very funny!

Gigi tells her mommy, "I don't want to go to school. I'm gonna miss you!"

"Yes, it's true," says Gigi's mommy. "School is starting for little big girls just like you. I will miss you, too!"

Gigi packs her lunch: A sandwich, an apple, and to drink a fruit punch. Gigi's feeling she's going to miss her mommy a great big bunch!

Gigi tells her mommy, "I don't want to go to school. I'm gonna miss you!"

"Yes, it's true," says Gigi's mommy. "School is starting for little big girls just like you. I will miss you, too!"

Gigi and her mommy arrive at school. Gigi's feeling she would rather be at the pool!

Gigi tells her mommy, "I don't want to go to school. I'm gonna miss you!"

"Yes, it's true," says Gigi's mommy. "School is starting for little big girls just like you. I will miss you, too!"

Gigi walks into class, ready to have a seat, when she sees a girl screaming, crying, and kicking her feet!

The girl pouts and shouts, "I don't want to go to school! I'm gonna miss you!"

"My name is Gigi. Yes, it's true. School is starting for little big girls just like me and you!"

"I know you're feeling afraid; I'll hold your hand and be your new friend!"

Gigi stops feeling sad. Helping someone else makes her feel glad!

Gigi tells her mommy, "I do want to go to school! Making new friends will be fun! I'm feeling excited to learn a ton. Being in school might even be cool, but I'm still gonna miss you!"

"Yes, it's true," says Gigi's mommy. "It's the first day of school for little big girls just like you… and I will miss you, too!"

The End

www.ingramcontent.com/pod-product-compliance
Lightning Source LLC
Chambersburg PA
CBHW041439040426
42453CB00021B/2467